BETSY AND GIULIO MAESTRO

ALL ABOARD OVERNIGHT

A BOOK OF COMPOUND WORDS

CLARION BOOKS

NEW YORK

In fond remembrance
of Ann Troy

Clarion Books
a Houghton Mifflin Company imprint
215 Park Avenue South, New York, NY 10003
Text copyright © 1992 by Betsy Maestro
Illustrations copyright © 1992 by Giulio Maestro

Library of Congress Cataloging-in-Publication Data

Maestro, Betsy.
   All aboard overnight : a book of compound words / by
Betsy Maestro ; illustrated by Giulio Maestro.
      p.   cm.
   Summary: Introduces a number of compound words, such as
suitcase, railroad, and tablecloth, through the story of a
family taking a train trip.
   ISBN 0-395-51120-8
   1. English language — Compound words — Juvenile
literature.   [1. English language — Compound words.]   I. Maestro,
Giulio, ill.   II. Title.
PE1175.M28   1992
428.1 — dc20   90-23987
                           CIP
                           AC

HOR 10 9 8 7 6 5 4 3 2 1

ABOUT COMPOUND WORDS

A compound word is a word made up of two smaller words. When the two words are put together, they make a new word with a new meaning. **Tablecloth** is a compound word. It is made up of two small words — **table** and **cloth**. The new word means a cloth for the table.

There are some other compound words in this book that are not in the text or story. They appear only in the pictures. See if you can find them. Here is a list of the words:

popcorn	**headphones**	**wastebasket**	**headrest**
flashlight	**teacup**	**highchair**	**pillowcase**
earring	**sunglasses**	**saltshaker**	**candlelight**

Check the **timetable**!

My **wristwatch** says it's getting late.

Mom and I grab our **suitcases**.
We're off to the **railroad** station.

We're just in time!
We rush **upstairs** as the **trainman** shouts, "All aboard!"

From **inside** the train, we wave at Daddy
through the **windowpane**.

The conductor asks for our tickets.
They're in Mom's **handbag**.

Mom buys a **newspaper** to read and then we're
on our way.

From my **armchair**, I can watch the **countryside** whizzing by.

At **lunchtime**, Mom and I look for the dining car.

Our **tablecloth** matches my shirt!
I use my **teaspoon** to eat chocolate pudding.

Later, we do some **sightseeing** in the lounge car.
Bright **sunshine** pours in through the big windows.

I get to take some **snapshots** with Mom's camera
as the train slows down along the **shoreline**.

In the **afternoon**, we write some **postcards**.
There's a **mailbox** right on the train!

From a high **overpass**, I can see **rooftops** below us.

At a busy station, some **workmen** are unloading a **boxcar**.

Soon it's **dinnertime**. We have my favorite —
meatballs and spaghetti!

When **nightfall** comes, I get ready for bed.
"We're **halfway** there," says Mom.

In the tiny **bathroom**, I put on my **nightgown**.

I use my **toothbrush** and **washcloth** at the sink.

At **bedtime**, we read a **storybook**.
The **lamplight** makes our room seem cozy.

Later, from up in my berth, I see a **farmhouse** standing
alone in the **moonlight**.

Overnight, while **everyone** sleeps, the train speeds over many miles.

When I wake up, it's **sunrise**. I **tiptoe** to the window.

When the dining car opens, we have **pancakes** and **oatmeal**. Yummy!

When the train slows down at the **crossroads**, I can read
the **signposts**.

Suddenly, the train zooms **into** an **underground** tunnel.
The darkness makes it seem like **nighttime** again.

Mom says, "We're almost there!"
She takes out her **hairbrush** to fix my hair.

My **backpack** is ready to go. I hold the **handrail** tightly until the train stops.

We hurry **into** the big station. At the top of the **stairway**, we see them.
"**Grandma**! **Grandpa**!" I shout. "We're here! We're here at last!"